The Mindful Mama

A 52 week journal for cultivating gratitude, strengthening your mental health, and decluttering your mind

Printed in the United States of America

First Printing, 2019

ISBN 9781653033218

For more information and resources, please visit www.drkatiegerst.com.

This Journal belongs to:

_____

_____

_____

_____

Date: _____

_____
_____
_____
_____
_____
_____
_____
_____
_____
_____
_____
_____
_____
_____
_____
_____
_____
_____
_____
_____
_____

This week's highs:	This week's lows:
1.	1.
2.	2.
3.	3.

On a scale of 1-10, how was your week? Circle your response.

1 - 2 - 3 - 4 - 5 - 6 - 7 - 8 - 9 - 10

Why did you rate it this way?

_____
_____
_____
_____
_____
_____

This week I am grateful for:

_____
_____
_____
_____
_____
_____

Task Checklist:

☐ _____   ☐ _____

☐ _____   ☐ _____

☐ _____   ☐ _____

Date: _____

_____
_____
_____
_____
_____
_____
_____
_____
_____
_____
_____
_____
_____
_____
_____
_____
_____
_____
_____
_____
_____
_____

This week's highs:	This week's lows:
1.	1.
2.	2.
3.	3.

On a scale of 1-10, how was your week? Circle your response.

1 - 2 - 3 - 4 - 5 - 6 - 7 - 8 - 9 - 10

Why did you rate it this way?

_____

_____

_____

_____

_____

_____

This week I am grateful for:

_____

_____

_____

_____

_____

_____

Task Checklist:

☐ _____   ☐ _____

☐ _____   ☐ _____

☐ _____   ☐ _____

Date: _____

_____
_____
_____
_____
_____
_____
_____
_____
_____
_____
_____
_____
_____
_____
_____
_____
_____
_____
_____
_____

This week's highs:	This week's lows:
1.	1.
2.	2.
3.	3.

On a scale of 1-10, how was your week? Circle your response.

$$1 - 2 - 3 - 4 - 5 - 6 - 7 - 8 - 9 - 10$$

Why did you rate it this way?

_____

_____

_____

_____

_____

_____

This week I am grateful for:

_____

_____

_____

_____

_____

_____

Task Checklist:

☐ _____   ☐ _____

☐ _____   ☐ _____

☐ _____   ☐ _____

Date: _____

_____
_____
_____
_____
_____
_____
_____
_____
_____
_____
_____
_____
_____
_____
_____
_____
_____
_____
_____
_____
_____
_____

This week's highs:	This week's lows:
1.	1.
2.	2.
3.	3.

On a scale of 1-10, how was your week? Circle your response.

$$1 - 2 - 3 - 4 - 5 - 6 - 7 - 8 - 9 - 10$$

Why did you rate it this way?

_____

_____

_____

_____

_____

_____

This week I am grateful for:

_____

_____

_____

_____

_____

_____

_____

Task Checklist:

☐ _____   ☐ _____

☐ _____   ☐ _____

☐ _____   ☐ _____

Date: _____

_____
_____
_____
_____
_____
_____
_____
_____
_____
_____
_____
_____
_____
_____
_____
_____
_____
_____
_____
_____
_____
_____
_____
_____

This week's highs:	This week's lows:
1.	1.
2.	2.
3.	3.

On a scale of 1-10, how was your week? Circle your response.

1 - 2 - 3 - 4 - 5 - 6 - 7 - 8 - 9 - 10

Why did you rate it this way?

_____

_____

_____

_____

_____

_____

_____

This week I am grateful for:

_____

_____

_____

_____

_____

_____

_____

Task Checklist:

☐ _____   ☐ _____

☐ _____   ☐ _____

☐ _____   ☐ _____

Date: _____

_____
_____
_____
_____
_____
_____
_____
_____
_____
_____
_____
_____
_____
_____
_____
_____
_____
_____
_____
_____
_____
_____

This week's highs:	This week's lows:
1.	1.
2.	2.
3.	3.

On a scale of 1-10, how was your week? Circle your response.

1 - 2 - 3 - 4 - 5 - 6 - 7 - 8 - 9 - 10

Why did you rate it this way?

_____

_____

_____

_____

_____

_____

This week I am grateful for:

_____

_____

_____

_____

_____

_____

_____

Task Checklist:

☐ _____   ☐ _____

☐ _____   ☐ _____

☐ _____   ☐ _____

Date: _____

_____
_____
_____
_____
_____
_____
_____
_____
_____
_____
_____
_____
_____
_____
_____
_____
_____
_____
_____
_____

This week's highs:	This week's lows:
1.	1.
2.	2.
3.	3.

On a scale of 1-10, how was your week? Circle your response.

$$1 - 2 - 3 - 4 - 5 - 6 - 7 - 8 - 9 - 10$$

Why did you rate it this way?

_____

_____

_____

_____

_____

_____

This week I am grateful for:

_____

_____

_____

_____

_____

_____

Task Checklist:

☐ _____   ☐ _____

☐ _____   ☐ _____

☐ _____   ☐ _____

Date: _____

_____
_____
_____
_____
_____
_____
_____
_____
_____
_____
_____
_____
_____
_____
_____
_____
_____
_____
_____
_____
_____
_____
_____

This week's highs:	This week's lows:
1.	1.
2.	2.
3.	3.

On a scale of 1-10, how was your week? Circle your response.

$$1 - 2 - 3 - 4 - 5 - 6 - 7 - 8 - 9 - 10$$

Why did you rate it this way?

_____

_____

_____

_____

_____

_____

This week I am grateful for:

_____

_____

_____

_____

_____

_____

Task Checklist:

☐ _____   ☐ _____

☐ _____   ☐ _____

☐ _____   ☐ _____

Date: _____

_____
_____
_____
_____
_____
_____
_____
_____
_____
_____
_____
_____
_____
_____
_____
_____
_____
_____
_____
_____
_____

This week's highs:	This week's lows:
1.	1.
2.	2.
3.	3.

On a scale of 1-10, how was your week? Circle your response.

$$1 - 2 - 3 - 4 - 5 - 6 - 7 - 8 - 9 - 10$$

Why did you rate it this way?

_____

_____

_____

_____

_____

_____

This week I am grateful for:

_____

_____

_____

_____

_____

_____

_____

Task Checklist:

☐ _____   ☐ _____

☐ _____   ☐ _____

☐ _____   ☐ _____

Date: _____

_____
_____
_____
_____
_____
_____
_____
_____
_____
_____
_____
_____
_____
_____
_____
_____
_____
_____
_____
_____
_____

This week's highs:	This week's lows:
1.	1.
2.	2.
3.	3.

On a scale of 1-10, how was your week? Circle your response.

1 - 2 - 3 - 4 - 5 - 6 - 7 - 8 - 9 - 10

Why did you rate it this way?

_____

_____

_____

_____

_____

_____

This week I am grateful for:

_____

_____

_____

_____

_____

_____

Task Checklist:

☐ _____   ☐ _____

☐ _____   ☐ _____

☐ _____   ☐ _____

_____
_____
_____
_____
_____
_____
_____
_____
_____
_____
_____
_____
_____
_____
_____
_____
_____
_____
_____
_____

This week's highs:	This week's lows:
1.	1.
2.	2.
3.	3.

On a scale of 1-10, how was your week? Circle your response.

$$1 - 2 - 3 - 4 - 5 - 6 - 7 - 8 - 9 - 10$$

Why did you rate it this way?

_____

_____

_____

_____

_____

_____

This week I am grateful for:

_____

_____

_____

_____

_____

_____

Task Checklist:

☐ _____   ☐ _____

☐ _____   ☐ _____

☐ _____   ☐ _____

Date: _____

_____
_____
_____
_____
_____
_____
_____
_____
_____
_____
_____
_____
_____
_____
_____
_____
_____
_____
_____
_____
_____

This week's highs:
  1.

  2.

  3.

This week's lows:
  1.

  2.

  3.

On a scale of 1-10, how was your week? Circle your response.

1 - 2 - 3 - 4 - 5 - 6 - 7 - 8 - 9 - 10

Why did you rate it this way?

_____

_____

_____

_____

_____

_____

This week I am grateful for:

_____

_____

_____

_____

_____

_____

Task Checklist:

☐ _____   ☐ _____

☐ _____   ☐ _____

☐ _____   ☐ _____

Date: _____

_____
_____
_____
_____
_____
_____
_____
_____
_____
_____
_____
_____
_____
_____
_____
_____
_____
_____
_____
_____
_____

This week's highs:	This week's lows:
1.	1.
2.	2.
3.	3.

On a scale of 1-10, how was your week? Circle your response.

1 - 2 - 3 - 4 - 5 - 6 - 7 - 8 - 9 - 10

Why did you rate it this way?

_____

_____

_____

_____

_____

_____

This week I am grateful for:

_____

_____

_____

_____

_____

_____

Task Checklist:

☐ _____   ☐ _____

☐ _____   ☐ _____

☐ _____   ☐ _____

Date: _____

_____
_____
_____
_____
_____
_____
_____
_____
_____
_____
_____
_____
_____
_____
_____
_____
_____
_____
_____
_____
_____

This week's highs:	This week's lows:
1.	1.
2.	2.
3.	3.

On a scale of 1-10, how was your week? Circle your response.

$$1 - 2 - 3 - 4 - 5 - 6 - 7 - 8 - 9 - 10$$

Why did you rate it this way?

_____

_____

_____

_____

_____

_____

This week I am grateful for:

_____

_____

_____

_____

_____

_____

_____

Task Checklist:

☐ _____   ☐ _____

☐ _____   ☐ _____

☐ _____   ☐ _____

Date: _____

_____
_____
_____
_____
_____
_____
_____
_____
_____
_____
_____
_____
_____
_____
_____
_____
_____
_____
_____
_____
_____
_____

This week's highs:	This week's lows:
1.	1.
2.	2.
3.	3.

On a scale of 1-10, how was your week? Circle your response.

1 - 2 - 3 - 4 - 5 - 6 - 7 - 8 - 9 - 10

Why did you rate it this way?

_____

_____

_____

_____

_____

_____

This week I am grateful for:

_____

_____

_____

_____

_____

_____

Task Checklist:

☐ _____ ☐ _____

☐ _____ ☐ _____

☐ _____ ☐ _____

Date: _____

_____
_____
_____
_____
_____
_____
_____
_____
_____
_____
_____
_____
_____
_____
_____
_____
_____
_____
_____
_____
_____

This week's highs:	This week's lows:
1.	1.
2.	2.
3.	3.

On a scale of 1-10, how was your week? Circle your response.

1 - 2 - 3 - 4 - 5 - 6 - 7 - 8 - 9 - 10

Why did you rate it this way?

_____

_____

_____

_____

_____

_____

This week I am grateful for:

_____

_____

_____

_____

_____

_____

Task Checklist:

☐ _____   ☐ _____

☐ _____   ☐ _____

☐ _____   ☐ _____

Date: _____

_____

_____

_____

_____

_____

_____

_____

_____

_____

_____

_____

_____

_____

_____

_____

_____

_____

_____

_____

This week's highs:
1.

2.

3.

This week's lows:
1.

2.

3.

On a scale of 1-10, how was your week? Circle your response.

$$1 - 2 - 3 - 4 - 5 - 6 - 7 - 8 - 9 - 10$$

Why did you rate it this way?

_____

_____

_____

_____

_____

_____

This week I am grateful for:

_____

_____

_____

_____

_____

_____

Task Checklist:

☐ _____   ☐ _____

☐ _____   ☐ _____

☐ _____   ☐ _____

Date: _____

_____
_____
_____
_____
_____
_____
_____
_____
_____
_____
_____
_____
_____
_____
_____
_____
_____
_____
_____
_____
_____

This week's highs:	This week's lows:
1.	1.
2.	2.
3.	3.

On a scale of 1-10, how was your week? Circle your response.

1 - 2 - 3 - 4 - 5 - 6 - 7 - 8 - 9 - 10

Why did you rate it this way?

_____

_____

_____

_____

_____

_____

This week I am grateful for:

_____

_____

_____

_____

_____

_____

Task Checklist:

☐ _____   ☐ _____

☐ _____   ☐ _____

☐ _____   ☐ _____

Date: _____

_____
_____
_____
_____
_____
_____
_____
_____
_____
_____
_____
_____
_____
_____
_____
_____
_____
_____
_____
_____

This week's highs:	This week's lows:
1.	1.
2.	2.
3.	3.

On a scale of 1-10, how was your week? Circle your response.

1 - 2 - 3 - 4 - 5 - 6 - 7 - 8 - 9 - 10

Why did you rate it this way?

_____

_____

_____

_____

_____

_____

This week I am grateful for:

_____

_____

_____

_____

_____

_____

Task Checklist:

☐ _____   ☐ _____

☐ _____   ☐ _____

☐ _____   ☐ _____

Date: _____

_____
_____
_____
_____
_____
_____
_____
_____
_____
_____
_____
_____
_____
_____
_____
_____
_____
_____
_____
_____

This week's highs:	This week's lows:
1.	1.
2.	2.
3.	3.

On a scale of 1-10, how was your week? Circle your response.

1 - 2 - 3 - 4 - 5 - 6 - 7 - 8 - 9 - 10

Why did you rate it this way?

_____

_____

_____

_____

_____

_____

This week I am grateful for:

_____

_____

_____

_____

_____

_____

Task Checklist:

☐ _____   ☐ _____

☐ _____   ☐ _____

☐ _____   ☐ _____

Date: _____

_____
_____
_____
_____
_____
_____
_____
_____
_____
_____
_____
_____
_____
_____
_____
_____
_____
_____
_____
_____
_____
_____

This week's highs:
  1.

  2.

  3.

This week's lows:
  1.

  2.

  3.

On a scale of 1-10, how was your week? Circle your response.

1 - 2 - 3 - 4 - 5 - 6 - 7 - 8 - 9 - 10

Why did you rate it this way?

_____

_____

_____

_____

_____

_____

This week I am grateful for:

_____

_____

_____

_____

_____

_____

Task Checklist:

☐ _____   ☐ _____

☐ _____   ☐ _____

☐ _____   ☐ _____

Date: _____

_____
_____
_____
_____
_____
_____
_____
_____
_____
_____
_____
_____
_____
_____
_____
_____
_____
_____
_____
_____

This week's highs:	This week's lows:
1.	1.
2.	2.
3.	3.

On a scale of 1-10, how was your week? Circle your response.

$$1 - 2 - 3 - 4 - 5 - 6 - 7 - 8 - 9 - 10$$

Why did you rate it this way?

_____

_____

_____

_____

_____

_____

This week I am grateful for:

_____

_____

_____

_____

_____

_____

Task Checklist:

☐ _____   ☐ _____

☐ _____   ☐ _____

☐ _____   ☐ _____

Date: _____

_____
_____
_____
_____
_____
_____
_____
_____
_____
_____
_____
_____
_____
_____
_____
_____
_____
_____
_____
_____
_____

This week's highs:	This week's lows:
1.	1.
2.	2.
3.	3.

On a scale of 1-10, how was your week? Circle your response.

1 - 2 - 3 - 4 - 5 - 6 - 7 - 8 - 9 - 10

Why did you rate it this way?

_____

_____

_____

_____

_____

_____

This week I am grateful for:

_____

_____

_____

_____

_____

_____

Task Checklist:

☐ _____   ☐ _____

☐ _____   ☐ _____

☐ _____   ☐ _____

Date: _____

_____
_____
_____
_____
_____
_____
_____
_____
_____
_____
_____
_____
_____
_____
_____
_____
_____
_____
_____
_____

This week's highs:	This week's lows:
1.	1.
2.	2.
3.	3.

On a scale of 1-10, how was your week? Circle your response.

$$1 - 2 - 3 - 4 - 5 - 6 - 7 - 8 - 9 - 10$$

Why did you rate it this way?

_____

_____

_____

_____

_____

_____

This week I am grateful for:

_____

_____

_____

_____

_____

_____

Task Checklist:

☐ _____   ☐ _____

☐ _____   ☐ _____

☐ _____   ☐ _____

Date: _____

_____
_____
_____
_____
_____
_____
_____
_____
_____
_____
_____
_____
_____
_____
_____
_____
_____
_____
_____
_____
_____
_____
_____

This week's highs:	This week's lows:
1.	1.
2.	2.
3.	3.

On a scale of 1-10, how was your week? Circle your response.

$$1 - 2 - 3 - 4 - 5 - 6 - 7 - 8 - 9 - 10$$

Why did you rate it this way?

_____

_____

_____

_____

_____

_____

This week I am grateful for:

_____

_____

_____

_____

_____

_____

Task Checklist:

☐ _____   ☐ _____

☐ _____   ☐ _____

☐ _____   ☐ _____

Date: _____

_____
_____
_____
_____
_____
_____
_____
_____
_____
_____
_____
_____
_____
_____
_____
_____
_____
_____
_____
_____
_____

This week's highs:	This week's lows:
1.	1.
2.	2.
3.	3.

On a scale of 1-10, how was your week? Circle your response.

1 - 2 - 3 - 4 - 5 - 6 - 7 - 8 - 9 - 10

Why did you rate it this way?

_____

_____

_____

_____

_____

_____

_____

This week I am grateful for:

_____

_____

_____

_____

_____

_____

_____

Task Checklist:

☐ _____   ☐ _____

☐ _____   ☐ _____

☐ _____   ☐ _____

Date: _____

_____
_____
_____
_____
_____
_____
_____
_____
_____
_____
_____
_____
_____
_____
_____
_____
_____
_____
_____
_____

This week's highs:	This week's lows:
1.	1.
2.	2.
3.	3.

On a scale of 1-10, how was your week? Circle your response.

$$1 - 2 - 3 - 4 - 5 - 6 - 7 - 8 - 9 - 10$$

Why did you rate it this way?

_____

_____

_____

_____

_____

_____

This week I am grateful for:

_____

_____

_____

_____

_____

_____

_____

Task Checklist:

☐ _____   ☐ _____

☐ _____   ☐ _____

☐ _____   ☐ _____

Date: _____

_____
_____
_____
_____
_____
_____
_____
_____
_____
_____
_____
_____
_____
_____
_____
_____
_____
_____
_____
_____
_____
_____

This week's highs:	This week's lows:
1.	1.
2.	2.
3.	3.

On a scale of 1-10, how was your week? Circle your response.

$$1 - 2 - 3 - 4 - 5 - 6 - 7 - 8 - 9 - 10$$

Why did you rate it this way?

_____

_____

_____

_____

_____

_____

This week I am grateful for:

_____

_____

_____

_____

_____

_____

Task Checklist:

☐ _____   ☐ _____

☐ _____   ☐ _____

☐ _____   ☐ _____

Date: _____

_____
_____
_____
_____
_____
_____
_____
_____
_____
_____
_____
_____
_____
_____
_____
_____
_____
_____
_____
_____
_____
_____

This week's highs:	This week's lows:
1.	1.
2.	2.
3.	3.

On a scale of 1-10, how was your week? Circle your response.

$$1 - 2 - 3 - 4 - 5 - 6 - 7 - 8 - 9 - 10$$

Why did you rate it this way?

_____

_____

_____

_____

_____

_____

_____

This week I am grateful for:

_____

_____

_____

_____

_____

_____

Task Checklist:

☐ _____   ☐ _____

☐ _____   ☐ _____

☐ _____   ☐ _____

Date: _____

_____
_____
_____
_____
_____
_____
_____
_____
_____
_____
_____
_____
_____
_____
_____
_____
_____
_____
_____
_____

This week's highs:	This week's lows:
1.	1.
2.	2.
3.	3.

On a scale of 1-10, how was your week? Circle your response.

$$1 - 2 - 3 - 4 - 5 - 6 - 7 - 8 - 9 - 10$$

Why did you rate it this way?

_____
_____
_____
_____
_____
_____
_____

This week I am grateful for:

_____
_____
_____
_____
_____
_____
_____

Task Checklist:

☐ _____   ☐ _____

☐ _____   ☐ _____

☐ _____   ☐ _____

Date: _____

_____
_____
_____
_____
_____
_____
_____
_____
_____
_____
_____
_____
_____
_____
_____
_____
_____
_____
_____
_____
_____
_____

This week's highs:	This week's lows:
1.	1.
2.	2.
3.	3.

On a scale of 1-10, how was your week? Circle your response.

1 - 2 - 3 - 4 - 5 - 6 - 7 - 8 - 9 - 10

Why did you rate it this way?

_____

_____

_____

_____

_____

_____

This week I am grateful for:

_____

_____

_____

_____

_____

_____

Task Checklist:

☐ _____ ☐ _____

☐ _____ ☐ _____

☐ _____ ☐ _____

Date: _____

_____
_____
_____
_____
_____
_____
_____
_____
_____
_____
_____
_____
_____
_____
_____
_____
_____
_____
_____
_____
_____

This week's highs:	This week's lows:
1.	1.
2.	2.
3.	3.

On a scale of 1-10, how was your week? Circle your response.

$$1 - 2 - 3 - 4 - 5 - 6 - 7 - 8 - 9 - 10$$

Why did you rate it this way?

_____
_____
_____
_____
_____
_____

This week I am grateful for:

_____
_____
_____
_____
_____
_____

Task Checklist:

☐ _____   ☐ _____

☐ _____   ☐ _____

☐ _____   ☐ _____

Date: _____

_____
_____
_____
_____
_____
_____
_____
_____
_____
_____
_____
_____
_____
_____
_____
_____
_____
_____
_____
_____
_____
_____

This week's highs:
  1.

  2.

  3.

This week's lows:
  1.

  2.

  3.

On a scale of 1-10, how was your week? Circle your response.

$$1 - 2 - 3 - 4 - 5 - 6 - 7 - 8 - 9 - 10$$

Why did you rate it this way?

_____

_____

_____

_____

_____

_____

This week I am grateful for:

_____

_____

_____

_____

_____

_____

Task Checklist:

☐ _____   ☐ _____

☐ _____   ☐ _____

☐ _____   ☐ _____

Date: _____

_____
_____
_____
_____
_____
_____
_____
_____
_____
_____
_____
_____
_____
_____
_____
_____
_____
_____
_____
_____
_____

This week's highs:
 1.

 2.

 3.

This week's lows:
 1.

 2.

 3.

On a scale of 1-10, how was your week? Circle your response.

$$1 - 2 - 3 - 4 - 5 - 6 - 7 - 8 - 9 - 10$$

Why did you rate it this way?

_____

_____

_____

_____

_____

_____

This week I am grateful for:

_____

_____

_____

_____

_____

_____

Task Checklist:

☐ _____   ☐ _____

☐ _____   ☐ _____

☐ _____   ☐ _____

Date: _____

_____
_____
_____
_____
_____
_____
_____
_____
_____
_____
_____
_____
_____
_____
_____
_____
_____
_____
_____
_____

This week's highs:	This week's lows:
1.	1.
2.	2.
3.	3.

On a scale of 1-10, how was your week? Circle your response.

1 - 2 - 3 - 4 - 5 - 6 - 7 - 8 - 9 - 10

Why did you rate it this way?

_____

_____

_____

_____

_____

_____

This week I am grateful for:

_____

_____

_____

_____

_____

_____

Task Checklist:

☐ _____ ☐ _____

☐ _____ ☐ _____

☐ _____ ☐ _____

Date: _____

_____
_____
_____
_____
_____
_____
_____
_____
_____
_____
_____
_____
_____
_____
_____
_____
_____
_____

This week's highs:	This week's lows:
1.	1.
2.	2.
3.	3.

On a scale of 1-10, how was your week? Circle your response.

1 - 2 - 3 - 4 - 5 - 6 - 7 - 8 - 9 - 10

Why did you rate it this way?

_____
_____
_____
_____
_____
_____
_____

This week I am grateful for:

_____
_____
_____
_____
_____
_____

Task Checklist:

☐ _____   ☐ _____
☐ _____   ☐ _____
☐ _____   ☐ _____

Date: _____

_____
_____
_____
_____
_____
_____
_____
_____
_____
_____
_____
_____
_____
_____
_____
_____
_____
_____
_____
_____
_____

This week's highs:	This week's lows:
1.	1.
2.	2.
3.	3.

On a scale of 1-10, how was your week? Circle your response.

$$1 - 2 - 3 - 4 - 5 - 6 - 7 - 8 - 9 - 10$$

Why did you rate it this way?

_____

_____

_____

_____

_____

_____

This week I am grateful for:

_____

_____

_____

_____

_____

_____

Task Checklist:

☐ _____   ☐ _____

☐ _____   ☐ _____

☐ _____   ☐ _____

Date: _____

_____
_____
_____
_____
_____
_____
_____
_____
_____
_____
_____
_____
_____
_____
_____
_____
_____
_____
_____
_____

This week's highs:	This week's lows:
1.	1.
2.	2.
3.	3.

On a scale of 1-10, how was your week? Circle your response.

1 - 2 - 3 - 4 - 5 - 6 - 7 - 8 - 9 - 10

Why did you rate it this way?

_____

_____

_____

_____

_____

_____

_____

This week I am grateful for:

_____

_____

_____

_____

_____

_____

Task Checklist:

☐ _____ ☐ _____

☐ _____ ☐ _____

☐ _____ ☐ _____

Date: _____

_____

_____

_____

_____

_____

_____

_____

_____

_____

_____

_____

_____

_____

_____

_____

_____

_____

_____

This week's highs:
  1.

  2.

  3.

This week's lows:
  1.

  2.

  3.

On a scale of 1-10, how was your week? Circle your response.

1 - 2 - 3 - 4 - 5 - 6 - 7 - 8 - 9 - 10

Why did you rate it this way?

_____

_____

_____

_____

_____

_____

_____

This week I am grateful for:

_____

_____

_____

_____

_____

_____

Task Checklist:

☐ _____   ☐ _____

☐ _____   ☐ _____

☐ _____   ☐ _____

Date: _____

_____
_____
_____
_____
_____
_____
_____
_____
_____
_____
_____
_____
_____
_____
_____
_____
_____
_____
_____
_____
_____

This week's highs:
1.

2.

3.

This week's lows:
1.

2.

3.

On a scale of 1-10, how was your week? Circle your response.

$$1 - 2 - 3 - 4 - 5 - 6 - 7 - 8 - 9 - 10$$

Why did you rate it this way?

_____

_____

_____

_____

_____

_____

This week I am grateful for:

_____

_____

_____

_____

_____

_____

Task Checklist:

☐ _____   ☐ _____

☐ _____   ☐ _____

☐ _____   ☐ _____

Date: _____

_____
_____
_____
_____
_____
_____
_____
_____
_____
_____
_____
_____
_____
_____
_____
_____
_____
_____
_____

This week's highs:	This week's lows:
1.	1.
2.	2.
3.	3.

On a scale of 1-10, how was your week? Circle your response.

1 - 2 - 3 - 4 - 5 - 6 - 7 - 8 - 9 - 10

Why did you rate it this way?

_____
_____
_____
_____
_____
_____

This week I am grateful for:

_____
_____
_____
_____
_____
_____

Task Checklist:

☐ _____   ☐ _____

☐ _____   ☐ _____

☐ _____   ☐ _____

Date: _____

_____
_____
_____
_____
_____
_____
_____
_____
_____
_____
_____
_____
_____
_____
_____
_____
_____
_____
_____
_____

This week's highs:
1.

2.

3.

This week's lows:
1.

2.

3.

On a scale of 1-10, how was your week? Circle your response.

1 - 2 - 3 - 4 - 5 - 6 - 7 - 8 - 9 - 10

Why did you rate it this way?

_____
_____
_____
_____
_____
_____

This week I am grateful for:

_____
_____
_____
_____
_____
_____

Task Checklist:

☐ _____   ☐ _____

☐ _____   ☐ _____

☐ _____   ☐ _____

Date: _____

_____

_____

_____

_____

_____

_____

_____

_____

_____

_____

_____

_____

_____

_____

_____

_____

_____

_____

_____

This week's highs:
  1.

  2.

  3.

This week's lows:
  1.

  2.

  3.

On a scale of 1-10, how was your week? Circle your response.

$$1 - 2 - 3 - 4 - 5 - 6 - 7 - 8 - 9 - 10$$

Why did you rate it this way?

_____

_____

_____

_____

_____

_____

This week I am grateful for:

_____

_____

_____

_____

_____

_____

Task Checklist:

☐ _____   ☐ _____

☐ _____   ☐ _____

☐ _____   ☐ _____

Date: _____

_____
_____
_____
_____
_____
_____
_____
_____
_____
_____
_____
_____
_____
_____
_____
_____
_____
_____

This week's highs:	This week's lows:
1.	1.
2.	2.
3.	3.

On a scale of 1-10, how was your week? Circle your response.

1 - 2 - 3 - 4 - 5 - 6 - 7 - 8 - 9 - 10

Why did you rate it this way?

_____

_____

_____

_____

_____

_____

This week I am grateful for:

_____

_____

_____

_____

_____

_____

Task Checklist:

☐ _____   ☐ _____

☐ _____   ☐ _____

☐ _____   ☐ _____

Date: _____

_____
_____
_____
_____
_____
_____
_____
_____
_____
_____
_____
_____
_____
_____
_____
_____
_____
_____
_____
_____
_____
_____

This week's highs:
  1.

  2.

  3.

This week's lows:
  1.

  2.

  3.

On a scale of 1-10, how was your week? Circle your response.

1 - 2 - 3 - 4 - 5 - 6 - 7 - 8 - 9 - 10

Why did you rate it this way?

_____

_____

_____

_____

_____

_____

This week I am grateful for:

_____

_____

_____

_____

_____

_____

Task Checklist:

☐ _____   ☐ _____

☐ _____   ☐ _____

☐ _____   ☐ _____

Date: _____

_____
_____
_____
_____
_____
_____
_____
_____
_____
_____
_____
_____
_____
_____
_____
_____
_____
_____
_____
_____
_____

This week's highs:	This week's lows:
1.	1.
2.	2.
3.	3.

On a scale of 1-10, how was your week? Circle your response.

1 - 2 - 3 - 4 - 5 - 6 - 7 - 8 - 9 - 10

Why did you rate it this way?

_____

_____

_____

_____

_____

_____

This week I am grateful for:

_____

_____

_____

_____

_____

_____

Task Checklist:

☐ _____   ☐ _____

☐ _____   ☐ _____

☐ _____   ☐ _____

Date: _____

_____
_____
_____
_____
_____
_____
_____
_____
_____
_____
_____
_____
_____
_____
_____
_____
_____
_____
_____
_____

This week's highs:	This week's lows:
1.	1.
2.	2.
3.	3.

On a scale of 1-10, how was your week? Circle your response.

$$1 - 2 - 3 - 4 - 5 - 6 - 7 - 8 - 9 - 10$$

Why did you rate it this way?

_____

_____

_____

_____

_____

_____

This week I am grateful for:

_____

_____

_____

_____

_____

_____

Task Checklist:

☐ _____   ☐ _____

☐ _____   ☐ _____

☐ _____   ☐ _____

Date: _____

_____
_____
_____
_____
_____
_____
_____
_____
_____
_____
_____
_____
_____
_____
_____
_____
_____
_____
_____
_____

This week's highs:	This week's lows:
1.	1.
2.	2.
3.	3.

On a scale of 1-10, how was your week? Circle your response.

1 - 2 - 3 - 4 - 5 - 6 - 7 - 8 - 9 - 10

Why did you rate it this way?

_____
_____
_____
_____
_____
_____

This week I am grateful for:

_____
_____
_____
_____
_____
_____

Task Checklist:

☐ _____   ☐ _____

☐ _____   ☐ _____

☐ _____   ☐ _____

Date: _____

_____
_____
_____
_____
_____
_____
_____
_____
_____
_____
_____
_____
_____
_____
_____
_____
_____
_____
_____
_____
_____

This week's highs:
  1.

  2.

  3.

This week's lows:
  1.

  2.

  3.

On a scale of 1-10, how was your week? Circle your response.

$$1 - 2 - 3 - 4 - 5 - 6 - 7 - 8 - 9 - 10$$

Why did you rate it this way?

_____
_____
_____
_____
_____
_____

This week I am grateful for:

_____
_____
_____
_____
_____
_____

Task Checklist:

☐ _____   ☐ _____

☐ _____   ☐ _____

☐ _____   ☐ _____

Date: _____

_____
_____
_____
_____
_____
_____
_____
_____
_____
_____
_____
_____
_____
_____
_____
_____
_____
_____
_____

This week's highs:
  1.

  2.

  3.

This week's lows:
  1.

  2.

  3.

On a scale of 1-10, how was your week? Circle your response.

1 - 2 - 3 - 4 - 5 - 6 - 7 - 8 - 9 - 10

Why did you rate it this way?

_____

_____

_____

_____

_____

_____

_____

This week I am grateful for:

_____

_____

_____

_____

_____

_____

_____

Task Checklist:

☐ _____   ☐ _____

☐ _____   ☐ _____

☐ _____   ☐ _____

Date: _____

_____
_____
_____
_____
_____
_____
_____
_____
_____
_____
_____
_____
_____
_____
_____
_____
_____
_____
_____

This week's highs:
  1.

  2.

  3.

This week's lows:
  1.

  2.

  3.

On a scale of 1-10, how was your week? Circle your response.

1 - 2 - 3 - 4 - 5 - 6 - 7 - 8 - 9 - 10

Why did you rate it this way?

_____

_____

_____

_____

_____

_____

This week I am grateful for:

_____

_____

_____

_____

_____

_____

Task Checklist:

☐ _____   ☐ _____

☐ _____   ☐ _____

☐ _____   ☐ _____

Date: _____

_____
_____
_____
_____
_____
_____
_____
_____
_____
_____
_____
_____
_____
_____
_____
_____
_____
_____
_____
_____
_____

This week's highs:	This week's lows:
1.	1.
2.	2.
3.	3.

On a scale of 1-10, how was your week? Circle your response.

$$1 - 2 - 3 - 4 - 5 - 6 - 7 - 8 - 9 - 10$$

Why did you rate it this way?

_____

_____

_____

_____

_____

_____

This week I am grateful for:

_____

_____

_____

_____

_____

_____

Task Checklist:

☐ _____   ☐ _____

☐ _____   ☐ _____

☐ _____   ☐ _____

Made in the USA
Middletown, DE
14 September 2022

10426153R00060